FOSSIL HUNTING

First published in 2002 by
Grolier Educational
Sherman Turnpike
Danbury, Connecticut 06816
© Quartz Editions 2002

Library of Congress Cataloging-in-Publication Data
Extinct species.
         p. cm.
   Contents: v. 1. Why extinction occurs - - v. 2. Prehistoric animal life - - v. 3. Fossil
hunting - - v. 4. Extinct mammals - - v. 5. Extinct birds - - v. 6 Extinct underwater life - -
v. 7. Extinct reptiles and amphibians - - v. 8. Extinct invertebrates and plants - - v. 9.
Hominids - - v. 10. Atlas of extinction.
   Summary: Examines extinct species, including prehistoric man, and discusses why
extinction happens, as well as how information is gathered on species that existed
before humans evolved.
ISBN 0-7172-5564-6 (set) - - ISBN 0-7172-5565-4 (v. 1) - - ISBN 0-7172-5566-2 (v. 2)
- - ISBN 0-7172-5567-0 (v. 3) - - ISBN 0-7172-5568-9 (v. 4) - - ISBN 0-7172-5569-7 (v.
5) - - ISBN 0-7172-5570-0 (v. 6) - - ISBN 0-7172-5571-9 (v. 7) - - ISBN 0-7172-5572-7
(v. 8) - - ISBN 0-7172-5573-5 (v. 9) - - ISBN 0-7172-5574-3 (v. 10)
   1. Extinction (Biology) - - Juvenile literature. 2. Extinct animals - - Juvenile literature.
[1. Extinction (Biology) 2. Extinct animals.] I. Grolier Educational.

   QH78 .E88 2002
   578.68 - - dc21   2001055702

Produced by Quartz Editions
Premier House
112 Station Road
Edgware HA8 7BJ
UK

EDITORIAL DIRECTOR: Tamara Green
CREATIVE DIRECTOR: Marilyn Franks
PRINCIPAL ILLUSTRATOR: Neil Lloyd
CONTRIBUTING ILLUSTRATORS: Tony Gibbons, Helen Jones
EDITORIAL CONTRIBUTOR: Graham Coleman

Reprographics by Mullis Morgan, London
Printed in Belgium by Proost

ACKNOWLEDGMENTS

The publishers wish to thank the following for supplying
photographic images for this volume.

Front & back cover t SPL/J.Baum & D.Angus

Page 1t SPL/J.Baum & D.Angus;
p3t SPL/J.Baum & D.Angus; p8tr NHM; p9t NHM;
p10tl NHM; p10b NHM; p13bl NHPA/A.N.T.;
p13r NHPA/R.Tidman; p17t NHPA/B.Coster;
p18tr NHM; p27tl MEPL; p27tc MEPL;
p29tl NHM; p29br NHM; p31tl NHM; p31bl NHM;
p31r NHM/J.Sibbick; p32bl NHPA/D.Heuclin;
p33tc NHPA/R.Tidman; p33br NHPA/K.Schafer;
p34tr NHPA/K.Schafer; p39tl NHM;
p41tc NHPA/D.Heuclin; p41r NHPA/D.Heuclin;
p43tc NHM; p43br MEPL; p45tl NHPA/K.Schafer;
p45br MEPL.

Abbreviations: Mary Evans Picture Library (MEPL); Natural
History Museum (NHM);Natural History Photographic
Agency (NHPA); Science Photo Library (SPL); bottom (b);
center (c); left (l); right (r); top (t).

EXTINCT SPECIES

FOSSIL HUNTING

GROLIER EDUCATIONAL

SHERMAN TURNPIKE, DANBURY, CONNECTICUT 06816

MAKING BEDS
Turn to pages 8-9 to find out what happens to dead flora and fauna over long periods of time.

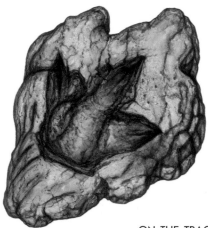

ON THE TRACK
In addition to looking for fossilized bones, paleontologists also hope to find signs of tracks, as outlined on pages 12-13.

BATTLING OVER BONES
Find out which 19th-century fossil hunters fought over bones by turning to pages 26-27.

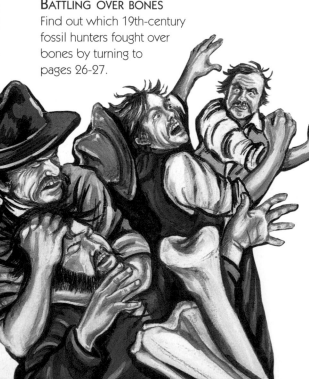

CONTENTS

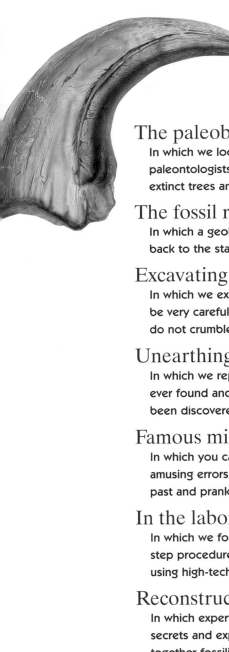

NAMED AFTER ITS FINDER
Turn to pages 24-25 to find out who discovered the claw, *left*, in a clay pit and the animal it came from.

SHARK'S TOOTH PURCHASED FROM FOSSIL SHOP, JULY 2000

MAMMOTH'S TOOTH UPPER MOLAR, FOUND IN PLEISTOCENE ROCKS

COPROLITE FROM LOWER JURASSIC STRATA

A GREAT HOBBY
Many superb fossil specimens are in the hands of private collectors, as outlined on pages 18-19.

ENTIRELY BY CHANCE
Read about the very surprising find made by the Australian farmer *above* on pages 24-25.

DIG THIS!
Find out what is involved when paleontologists start to dig by turning to pages 32-33.

PLANTS FROM THE PAST
Earth's prehistoric flora may never bloom again, but paleobotanists have preserved some for posterity, as described on pages 28-29.

INTRODUCTION

MYSTERY BONE
When Sir Robert Plot found this strange bone in the 17th century, he puzzled over what sort of extinct animal it might have come from. Would *you* have had any idea?

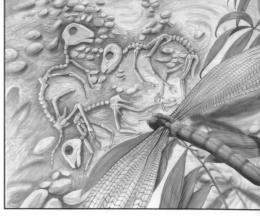

EXTINCT BABIES
When paleontologists find the skeletal remains of baby dinosaurs, they are especially thrilled because so few of their fossils have survived.

Many people think of fossils only in terms of skeletal remains. They are wrong, however. On the desk of the editor of this book, for example, there is a most unusual paperweight. It looks just like a piece of rock but is in fact a genuine lump of coprolites, the scientific word for fossilized dung. As authenticated by a paleontologist, it was excreted by a carnivorous dinosaur about 150 million years ago, way back in Jurassic times, and bought in the year 2000A.D. in a fossil shop.

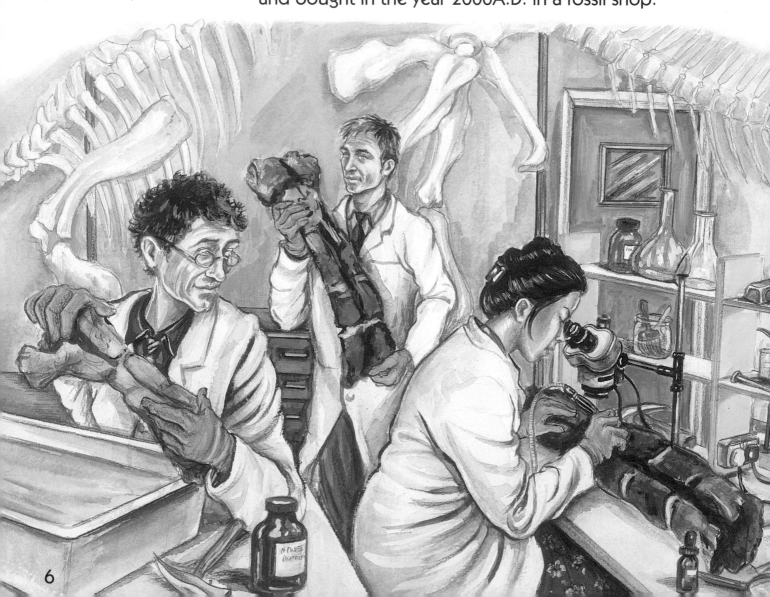

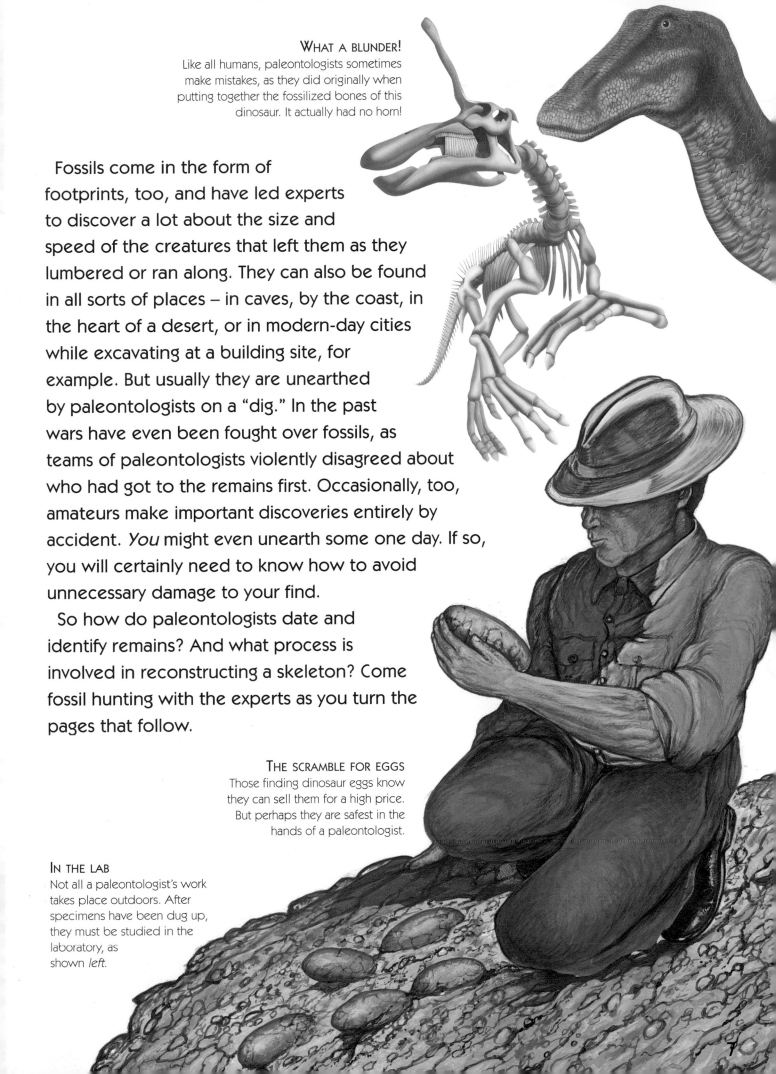

WHAT A BLUNDER!
Like all humans, paleontologists sometimes
make mistakes, as they did originally when
putting together the fossilized bones of this
dinosaur. It actually had no horn!

Fossils come in the form of
footprints, too, and have led experts
to discover a lot about the size and
speed of the creatures that left them as they
lumbered or ran along. They can also be found
in all sorts of places – in caves, by the coast, in
the heart of a desert, or in modern-day cities
while excavating at a building site, for
example. But usually they are unearthed
by paleontologists on a "dig." In the past
wars have even been fought over fossils, as
teams of paleontologists violently disagreed about
who had got to the remains first. Occasionally, too,
amateurs make important discoveries entirely by
accident. *You* might even unearth some one day. If so,
you will certainly need to know how to avoid
unnecessary damage to your find.

So how do paleontologists date and
identify remains? And what process is
involved in reconstructing a skeleton? Come
fossil hunting with the experts as you turn the
pages that follow.

THE SCRAMBLE FOR EGGS
Those finding dinosaur eggs know
they can sell them for a high price.
But perhaps they are safest in the
hands of a paleontologist.

IN THE LAB
Not all a paleontologist's work
takes place outdoors. After
specimens have been dug up,
they must be studied in the
laboratory, as
shown *left*.

7

FOSSIL FORMATION

Paleontologists regularly find the remains of animals that died thousands or even millions of years ago. But not all organisms become fossilized. So why do some specimens become preserved? And what processes do they undergo during fossilization?

EMBEDDED IN ROCK
The fossil *above* is of an *Archaeopteryx* (ARK-EE-OPT-ER-IKS), an ancestor of today's birds found in Late Jurassic strata in Germany. Only five such specimens have been unearthed so far.

Fossils provide us with valuable clues to the kind of life forms that lived in ancient times. But fossilization is not a guaranteed process. The vast majority of creatures simply decay so that no trace of their existence remains. For a fossil to be formed, a whole chain of favorable events has to occur.

Ideally, a dead animal's body will quickly become buried in soft sediments, such as sand and mud, and its bones will not be damaged by harsh weather.

The flesh on its body then decomposes, and the animal's skeleton sinks below the surface of the earth.

LAYER ON LAYER

Over a long period of time, sometimes millions of years, layers of sand and mud form over the remains of bones and teeth. And gradually, as the lower layers are crushed beneath the weight of all the material above, they harden and turn into rock.

As this happens, water and minerals in the rock slowly replace the original chemical makeup of the animal's bones; and it is this ongoing process that is known as fossilization.

A fossilized bone is in fact a rocklike copy of the original, but much heavier because any natural holes have been filled in.

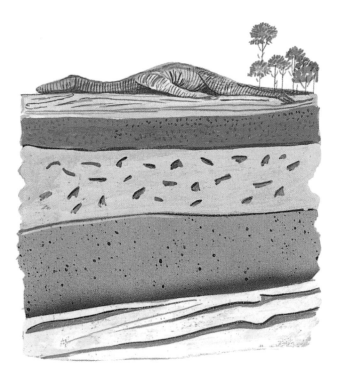

DEATH OF A DINOSAUR – STAGE 1
The dinosaur was killed by a predator that ate most of its skin, flesh, and inner organs. What soft tissue remained gradually decomposed.

STAGE 2
The dinosaur's skeleton gradually became covered in many layers of sand and mud. Lower strata slowly turned to rock.

TURNED TO COAL
This illustration features an artist's reconstruction of a typical Carboniferous forest 300 million years ago. When it died, such vegetation fossilized and turned into the deposits of coal that are now mined and used by industry.

A SOFTER TOUCH

It is not only an animal's bones and teeth, however, that may become preserved, even if only temporarily. Mummification, for example, is the natural drying of an organism so that some of its soft tissue is left intact. It is not a complete process, however, but a step toward fossilization.

In a far longer-lasting process, meanwhile, when frogs or insects became trapped in tree resin millions of years ago, this substance then hardened around them, so that over millions of years the skin, body organs, and skeletons of these creatures remained in almost perfect condition within the amber that had formed.

STAGE 3
Over time the dinosaur skeleton disintegrated and was forced upward. Hard minerals then replaced chemicals in the bones.

STAGE 4
One hundred and fifty million years after the remains had turned to stone, some of the fossilized bones were found by a paleontologist.

VISITING A FOSSIL SITE

In what sort of places are paleontologists usually successful in unearthing fossils? And what do these sites look like while a dig is underway? If you are lucky enough, you may be able to arrange an outing to a fossil site.

Some areas where numerous prehistoric remains have been discovered are now preserved as working museums where visitors are welcome to observe paleontologists and their assistants as they go about trying to unearth further finds.

One of the most exciting of these is Dinosaur National Monument, which straddles the states of Utah and Colorado. It was originally created in 1915 to preserve one of the world's great fossil sites, where remains of nearly every known dinosaur from Jurassic times have now been dug up.

Today visitors are overwhelmed to see around 2,000 dinosaur bones poking out from a huge sandstone wall, and at certain times of year they are permitted to view teams of paleontologists carefully removing newly discovered specimens.

CHIPPING AWAY
The photograph *left* shows a professional paleontologist trying to unearth a fossil find at a major site.

LOOKING FOR ANCESTORS
The team of paleontologists *below* are caught on camera as they search a fossil site for evidence of possible Neanderthal habitation.

Sometimes there will be frenetic activity. Paleontologists in hard hats may be climbing scaffolding specially put up so they can get at fossil deposits at a high elevation. Others may be working in teams to remove certain remains. Some will be taking notes, while a photographer makes a visual record of the find. Assistants may be wrapping and then packing bones before they are lifted by cranes for transport to a laboratory for study. But of course, no member of the public would be allowed anywhere near a spot where dynamite is being used to help remove a specimen.

Visitors can also see the laboratory where fossils are cleaned and preserved, and can attend regular talks about the dinosaur fossils or join guided tours of the park, which extends to 200,000 acres in all. But such occasions are not fossil free-for-alls, and visitors are courteously reminded not to take any natural object from the park, be it a fossil or a flower, nor to interfere with the digging process.

Another of the world's most spectacular prehistoric fossil sites is the La Brea tar pits of California. During the last Ice Age, between 10,000 and 40,000 years ago, many extinct animals, such as saber-toothed tigers, giant sloths, and mammoths, roamed what is now downtown Los Angeles, but large numbers of them became trapped in tar.

Then they perished in the gooey asphalt; but the plus side for 21st-century humans is that the tar preserved their remains. Indeed, since 1906 over three million fossils, including more than 650 species of animals and plants, have been recovered.

EASY PICKINGS

From an observation deck the public can sometimes watch paleontologists at work in a pit and see up to 25 large, 30,000-year-old fossils removed each day the site is open.

Removing bones from this site usually proves very much easier than elsewhere because the sludge has prevented them from becoming brittle, and they remain intact. Whether or not finds will be made on particular days is not in question. Instead, paleontologists wonder which sort of prehistoric species one day's dig will bring forth.

Visitors can also see remains being cleaned in the fossil preparation laboratory at nearby Page Museum, which houses many of the tar pits' fossils. But La Brea pits will never yield hominid material because our early ancestors did not reach North America until 8,000 years after the tar took its victims.

If you cannot personally get to a fossil site, however, you may be able to view one using Internet facilities. The Illinois State Museum, for example, provides information about a central Missouri cave at www.museum.state.il.us/exhibits/larson/cave_visit

On this Internet site you are invited to take a trip back in time to 16,000 years ago and visit an ancient cave. In the company of experts you can study the bones that have been found there, among them remains of short-faced bears, dire wolves, and peccaries.

A number of natural history museums also sometimes invite amateurs to pay to join a dig and obtain valuable field experience. Participants have assisted with unearthing skeletons at the huge Dinosaur Provincial Park area, for example, which has been designated a World Heritage Site because of the wealth of fossils found there.

TRACKS AND TRAILS

Some fossilized animal remains do not take the form of body parts at all. Most of them are footprints made when creatures stepped onto muddy ground, which then became set in stone. Surprisingly, too, sometimes scientists even find prehistoric animal dung.

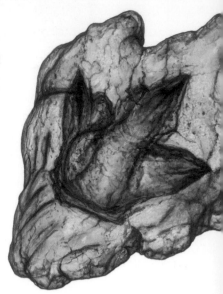

For centuries, whenever people found the fossilized footprints of large animals, they assumed they must have been left by an ancient race of giant humans who perhaps existed millions of years ago. But in time they began to notice other prints left by what must have been smaller extinct creatures, and eventually, a whole new branch of paleontology was launched. Known as paleoichnology (PAL-EE-OH-IK-NOL-OJ-EE), it involves the study of marks left by animals of bygone eras and their relation to size and behavior patterns.

Fossilized trackways reveal, for instance, that some animals would migrate in large numbers, protecting their young at the center of the herd as they wandered on.

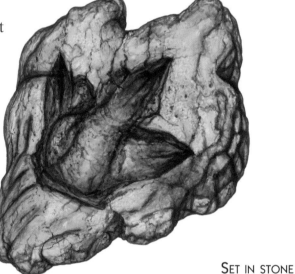

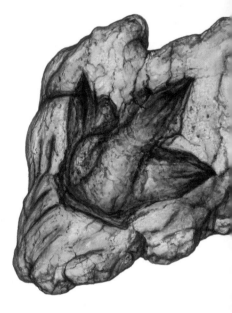

SET IN STONE
From fossilized footprints, such as those illustrated across this page, paleontologists can assess such factors as how many toes the creature had, when it lived, its likely weight and size, if it was part of a herd, whether it was bipedal or walked on all fours, the length of its stride, and its speed. Large numbers of sauropod footprints, for example, provide evidence that these massive dinosaurs were quadrupeds when on the move but would rear up on two legs only to feed from the treetops. Can you guess what sort of animal may have left the trail shown here?

But how did such footprints come to be preserved over so many millions of years? Initially, animals must have walked over soft ground, making deep impressions in the mud. The earth then hardened in a dry climate, and over countless years another layer formed over it. If the terrain remained undisturbed by any geological upheaval, these two distinct layers would have transformed into a sort of protective rock cast, so that when they broke apart, the original print was still there.

It is not always possible for paleoichnologists to identify the exact species that left a particular trackway. But they will usually be able to identify the sort of creature that would have left certain types of footprints by comparing the prints with those of other creatures of today. Fossilized footprints may also provide an indication of the sort of soil in which they were made.

CALCULATING SPEED

Astonishingly, too, scientists are even able to calculate the rate at which extinct animals were probably able to run by examining their tracks. On the whole, heavier species only lumbered along.

Those dinosaurs that weighed up to 50 tons – the long-necked sauropods, for example – left tracks that are very deep and close together. Smaller, lighter dinosaurs, however, have left tracks that are about 6 feet apart, pointing to a rapid pace. Indeed, paleontologists estimate that a dinosaur like the theropod *Dromiceiomimus* (DROM-IK-<u>EYE</u>-OH-<u>MEYE</u>-MUS) could run at a rapid 40 miles per hour.

MORE CLUES

Experts can also tell a lot about what extinct creatures ate from another type of trace fossil. Indeed, if they manage to find an extinct animal's droppings or dung, known as coprolites, scientific analysis of these hard fossils may reveal if that animal was a carnivore. Scientists can even tell the type of plants a herbivore ate from examination of its coprolites.

SIZING UP
The human hand in the photograph *above* shows the size of a dinosaur footprint unearthed in Spain.

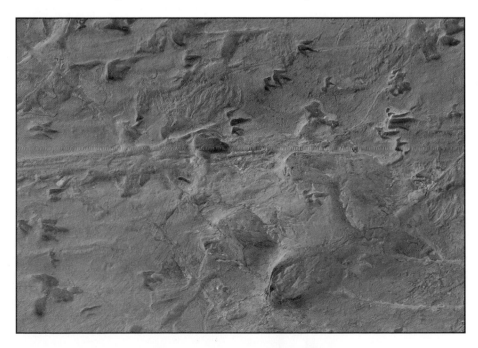

IN HOT PURSUIT
The fossilized dinosaur tracks *left* are 100 million years old and were made by a predator chasing its prey across a river bed in what is now Lark Quarry Park, Queensland, Australia.

CAVE SITES

Fossils of a wide variety of species have been found deep within caves. But not all these creatures lived in caves. Some may have been killed and taken there to be eaten by our distant ancestors, for instance, whose remains have been discovered in caves, too.

Some of the most important discoveries concerning the way in which our ancestors lived have been made in caves, where early hominids sheltered, cooked, ate, and slept. Exploration of the Shanidar caves in northern Iraq, for example, has provided evidence of a Neanderthal burial. Indeed, analysis of the fossilized bones of a man aged between 35 and 40 has shown he had sustained many serious, long-term injuries. This suggests that thousands of years ago he was probably looked after by a caring community. There is evidence, too, from other Neanderthal remains that a ritual burial ceremony of some kind must have taken place, which seems to point to belief in an afterlife.

The Sterkfontein caves of South Africa have also been among the most popular for paleontologists to explore, and hundreds of early hominid and animal fossils have been unearthed there, the oldest dating back three million years. Some of the earliest known stone tools have been discovered there, too. So perhaps it is not surprising the site has now become a major tourist attraction, although the exact location of some of the caves is kept secret to protect them from vandals.

HIDE-AND-SEEK
In prehistoric times our ancestors often hid in caves like the one shown *left* to avoid wild beasts, which is why paleoanthropologists now seek early human remains in this sort of environment.

WELL PRESERVED
This illustration shows a Neanderthal skull, discovered inside a cave. The atmosphere there kept it in good condition.

Another South African site, known as the Cave of Hearths, provides evidence that the earliest use of fire by our distant ancestors, as far as current knowledge permits, took place in this region.

The Naracoorte caves of South Australia, meanwhile, have yielded the fossilized remains of more than 100 different species, many of them long extinct, including giant prehistoric kangaroos and enormous lizards.

UNDERGROUND ART
Scientists exploring the Chauvet caves of southern France in 1994 got lucky in another way. Here they found a large number of magnificent murals featuring charging rhinos, horses, muskoxen, mammoths, lions, aurochs, and even an owl and a leopard, all painted around 35,000 years ago, making this cave art more than twice the age of that already found at Lascaux, France, and Altamira, Spain. Footprints preserved as trace fossils on the floors of the Chauvet caves also show they

Fact file

- Among cave-dwelling animals was the great cave bear, which lived some 10,000 years ago. It was much bigger than any of today's bears and liked to hibernate in the relative safety of caves.

- *Gigantopithecus* (JEYE-GANT-OH-PITH-EEK-OOS) was a ten- foot-tall prehistoric ape whose remains have been found in Chinese caves.

- The Chauvet caves were named after one of their discoverers, J. M. Chauvet.

- A scientist who studies and explores caves is called a "speleologist."

- Caves are often a good source of fossils because remains are kept dry and undamaged in the warm, subterranean surroundings.

were used as dens by wild creatures. What is more, 147 bear skulls were found there, one balanced on a protruding rock, which shows the Chauvet caves must have been used by early humans, too.

PAST MASTERS
It took the talent of a 21st-century professional painter to produce this replica cave painting, which indicates how skilled some of our early ancestors must have been.

DATING FOSSILS

When paleontologists unearth fossilized bones or plants or have specimens brought to them, there are a number of techniques that can now be used to determine the age of such remains. How do these methods work, and how accurate are they?

Unless there has been some sort of upheaval causing layers of rock to become upturned, lower strata will always be the most ancient. So the dating of fossils in relative terms – that is, determining which fossils are older than others – depends on the age of the strata in which they are found.

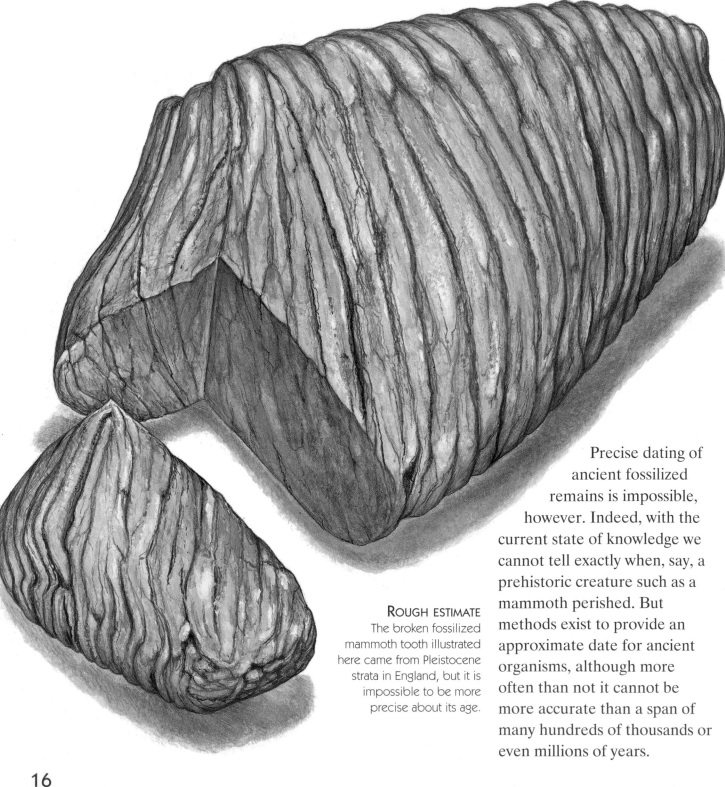

ROUGH ESTIMATE
The broken fossilized mammoth tooth illustrated here came from Pleistocene strata in England, but it is impossible to be more precise about its age.

Precise dating of ancient fossilized remains is impossible, however. Indeed, with the current state of knowledge we cannot tell exactly when, say, a prehistoric creature such as a mammoth perished. But methods exist to provide an approximate date for ancient organisms, although more often than not it cannot be more accurate than a span of many hundreds of thousands or even millions of years.

A GRAND AGE

This magnificent view of the Grand Canyon, Arizona, shows sedimentary rocks dating back 2 billion years. Fossils found in different layers give paleontologists an indication of the creatures living in the seas that covered this region at various points in time.

ELEMENTS OF AGING

In one method, for instance, the amount of a radioactive element known as carbon-14 can be measured to calculate the age of rock and therefore the age of any remains that are found in it.

While alive, both plant and animal life absorbed carbon-14 from the atmosphere. It is known that half the carbon-14 present in any substance decays every 5,568 years, so that the age of a fossil can be calculated from the amount of carbon-14 still present in it.

However, carbon dating can only be used with accuracy with material under 50,000 years old, which makes it excellent for working with human remains, but not with anything more ancient, such as 200-million-year-old dinosaur bones. For these remains other methods, such as measuring the amount of the element uranium-235 in a sample of nearby igneous rock, must be used.

Uranium-235 also has what is called a half-life, but one of 700 million years, which means it takes this long for half of it to decay before becoming transformed into the element lead-207. Scientists therefore measure how much uranium-235 and lead-207 are present in the nearby rock to calculate a fossil's age.

This process is known as radioisotope dating. However, uranium-235 is found only in igneous rock formed by volcanic eruptions, so that it cannot be used to date all ancient fossils, most of which are found among layers of sedimentary rock.

Other means of dating fossils focus on elements such as potassium-argon and rubidium-strontium. These elements decay extremely slowly – potassium-40, for instance, has a half-life of an incredible 1.3 billion years – so they have been used with the very earliest known fossilized remains.

Another method sometimes used for dating fossils relies on study of the magnetic fields in ancient rock layers, since scientists have discovered they changed a number of times during the course of our planet's long history.

But the hardest task of all is to estimate the so-called "existence span" of a species – that is, when it first appeared on our planet and when it finally became extinct. For how long, for example, did certain species of pterosaur rule the skies? When did woolly rhinos first evolve and eventually die out? The fossil record is so incomplete that it is inevitably a very imprecise process.

A GREAT HOBBY

Most amateurs become interested in paleontology through visiting natural history museums and marveling at the variety of prehistoric remains on display there. You, too, could start a private collection. It will require lots of enthusiasm but very little cost.

It always takes a considerable time to build a fossil collection of a reasonable size entirely from scratch, so it is good to bear in mind that you may not have many specimens for a while – unless, that is, you are lucky enough to be given a few to start with by relatives or friends who are themselves established amateur collectors. They, too, had to begin somewhere and so are sure to help and encourage you in your new interest.

BASIC EQUIPMENT

You will not need many tools at first, nor an elaborate display cabinet. Indeed, you could probably get by with just a few fine brushes for cleaning your specimens, a sieve for washing and retaining them, protective gloves and goggles, and a simple drawer for storage. Other items can be added at intervals. Beginners should avoid use of chemicals.

A NOBLE COLLECTION
One of the greatest collectors of stuffed specimens was Baron Lionel Walter Rothschild (1868-1937), shown in the portrait *above*. Many of these creatures, such as the quagga, are now extinct.

FINDERS KEEPERS?

The most exciting part of paleontology is always making finds. But whether or not you can keep them depends on local laws. Even if you unearth fossils on your own land, there may be a problem in some areas; and if you discover something in a national park, you are duty bound to advise the authorities.

AMMONITE
FOUND BY G. ROBERTS
ISLE OF WIGHT, 1998

GASTROPOD
CERITHIUM DUPLEX
FOUND IN EOCENE ROCKS

TRILOBITE
THIS SPECIMEN IS FROM
CAMBRIAN ROCKS

SHARK'S TOOTH
PURCHASED FROM FOSSIL
SHOP, JULY 2000

MAMMOTH'S TOOTH
UPPER MOLAR, FOUND IN
PLEISTOCENE ROCKS

COPROLITES
FROM LOWER
JURASSIC STRATA

ON DISPLAY
Accurate labeling
and safe storage of
fossils so they can best be
displayed are important for
amateurs and professionals alike.

In fact, you should not even attempt to remove it in case, when you do so, you damage the fossil. Museum curators always appreciate being told about fossil finds, and some have even given rewards for particularly spectacular specimens. They always discourage young people from fossil hunting on their own, however, because of the dangers involved and suggest joining groups led by at least one adult supervisor.

A guidebook to fossils will be extremely useful both at the start of your hobby and for years ahead. But what if you still get stuck with identifying what you have found?

You may be able to arrange an appointment with the appropriate department at a local natural history museum or perhaps seek the advice of a more advanced collector. At first, you will probably not be able to distinguish one type of trilobite from another, nor will a shark's tooth seem any different from a carnivorous dinosaur's. But with time you could become an expert in your own right. And once you have information about each specimen, remember to keep careful records.

SWAP SHOP
But how can you add to your collection without undue expense? You are bound to collect some identical fossil specimens and will no doubt start to hanker after others. It is then a good idea to exchange any you no longer require with fellow enthusiasts, who in turn will benefit by those you have unearthed in duplicate. Like some other junior collectors, you may also be able to request a particular fossil as a birthday gift. There are specialized fossil shops in some places and at certain museums, and many web sites list full descriptions and prices. But as usual, please ask parental permission.

DESERT EXPEDITIONS

Why do paleontologists so frequently organize expeditions to desert regions in spite of the unrelenting heat? What sort of finds have been unearthed in desert environments? And might fossils of unknown creatures still lie buried under the sands?

In a typical desert region few trees and plants grow, and wildlife is rare, other than at the site of an oasis because of the poor soil and lack of rainfall. The scorching heat of the day and the very cold nights, meanwhile, promote exposure of new rocks, which then crumble into sand. As a bonus, however, new fossilized remains frequently come to light.

IN THE BADLANDS

When we think of deserts, we generally imagine vast areas of sand; but there are also places where huge rocks have been sculptured by erosion to provide dramatic landscapes where, again, nothing grows. Geologists now refer to such areas as "badlands," and one part of South Dakota has even been designated the Badlands National Monument. Here countless fossils have been mined for over a century, and large numbers are continually exposed due to weathering.

VALLEY OF THE MOON

There are badlands in regions of South America, too; and in Argentina part of the Ischigualasto (ISH-IG-OO-AL-AST-OH) Provincial Park, now classed as a World Heritage site, has even been dubbed the Valley of the Moon due to its strange geological formations. Fossil finds here date mostly from Triassic times and include one of the earliest dinosaurs, *Eoraptor* (AY-OH-RAP-TOR). Therapsids – the first mammal-like reptiles – have been unearthed there, too.

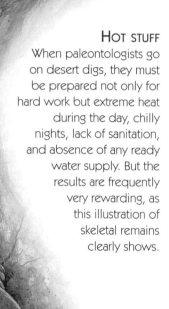

HOT STUFF
When paleontologists go on desert digs, they must be prepared not only for hard work but extreme heat during the day, chilly nights, lack of sanitation, and absence of any ready water supply. But the results are frequently very rewarding, as this illustration of skeletal remains clearly shows.

AN AMAZING SCENE

When Roy Chapman Andrews first glimpsed one of the most famous paleontological sites in the world at Flaming Cliffs in Mongolia's Gobi Desert in the 1920s, he was awestruck. Indeed, he wrote that:

"This is one of the most picturesque spots I have ever seen. From our tents, we looked down into a vast pink basin, studded with giant buttes like strange beasts, carved from sandstone. One of them we named 'dinosaur,' for it resembles a huge brontosaurus sitting on its haunches."

It proved to be a very suitable name because there in the heart of the desert, he and his team were to unearth valuable dinosaur remains, including the first ever dinosaur eggs ever found, some probably laid by a species with a neck frill, known as *Protoceratops* (PROH-TOH-SER-AH-TOPS.)

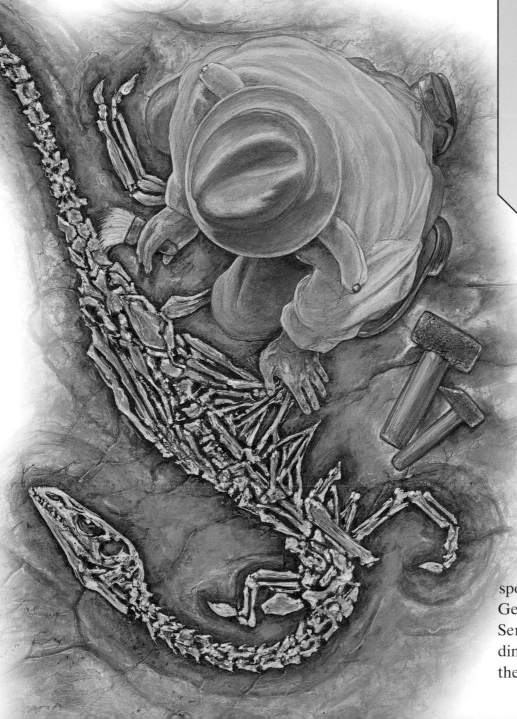

Fact file

● The American naturalist and explorer Roy Chapman Andrews found the first known fossilized dinosaur eggs and nesting sites in the pink sands of a region of Mongolia known as Flaming Cliffs in 1923. However, following this, because of political differences, scientists from the United States were not allowed to collect fossils in Mongolia until the late 1980s. Now, however, the Mongolian Academy of Sciences often works with paleontologists from the U.S. and elsewhere to cooperate with them on digs in the Gobi Desert. Any fossils found there have to remain the property of the Mongolian government. But they are sometimes sent on loan to other countries for study purposes.

IN THE SAHARA

More recently, in 2000 in a desert region of Africa one of the largest crocodilians ever to have existed was unearthed in Niger. Given the popular name Supercroc and 40 feet long, it lived about 110 million years ago and was discovered in the course of an expedition led by Professor Paul Sereno of the University of Chicago, partly sponsored by the National Geographic Society. Professor Sereno has also found many dinosaur remains in the Sahara, the world's largest desert.

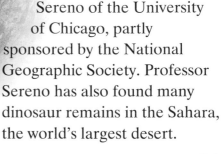

BY THE COAST

A huge number of prehistoric remains, ranging from ammonites to the almost complete skeletons of gigantic marine reptiles, have been found by beaches all over the world. Why, though, are so many coastal regions such rich fossil sites?

High, wave-washed cliffs and the shore lying beneath them are ideal places to look for fossils; but paleontologists always warn it is essential to have some knowledge of the local tides. So, as usual, the commonsense rules – not going on an unsupervised expedition, wearing a hard hat or helmet in case of falling stones, and waiting for nice weather – will apply. Fossil hunting by the sea is certainly a fascinating but potentially dangerous activity.

TO THE RESCUE

Indeed, in summer 2001 a team of coast guards was called in to assist at a moonlight operation. However, this time it was not a fossil hunter whose safety was at stake but the four 170-million-year-old dinosaur footprints lying at the bottom of a 70-foot-high cliff in northern England. Normally, such prints are left in place; but someone had sneakily tried to cut them out, so prompt action was required.

Two years previously, again on England's Yorkshire coast, amateur paleontologist Brian Foster had even found the remains of a marine mammal that had lain there ever since the creature sank to the bottom of the ocean 185 million years ago. This dolphinlike creature was discovered together with evidence of its last meal in a disused quarry, so that its fossilized bones had not been damaged by strong waves.

When in 1819 a local vicar, the Rvd. George Young, heard about the discovery of an ichthyosaur (IK-THEE-OH-SOR) by the coast near Whitby, England, he wrote that he very much regretted learning that:

"... creatures, all beautiful and interesting, should [have occupied] our globe throughout long ages, without any intelligent creatures to enjoy the scene."

ABOUT TO BE WASHED UP
One of the excitements of fossil hunting by the sea is that further remains are always being washed ashore. Next week there may be many more fossils to be found.

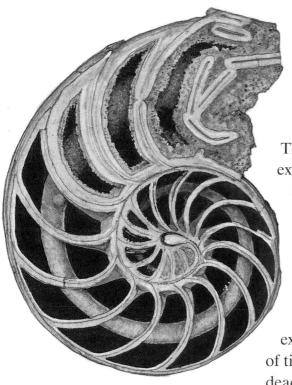

They even include fossils of extinct species of rhinos, early horses, and camels.

EXPOSED AT LAST

The usual pattern of events was that the bottom of a former shallow ocean became exposed over a huge expanse of time. The bodies of many dead land creatures were also frequently washed down to the sea by flowing rivers. Landslides also caused animals to be cast out to sea, where they drowned. But some corpses were tossed back shore by powerful waves.

Lincoln County on the coast of Oregon is another example of a fossil-rich site where petrified wood from prehistoric species of pine, myrtle, and alder trees is regularly unearthed or found lying completely exposed on the beaches. Here local laws permit such fossils to be collected in some spots and then traded with other collectors, but they may not be sold; nor may picks be used to remove them from seawalls.

However, paleontologists would argue that finding their fossils, whether by the sea or inland, goes some way toward making up for this.

In the county of Dorset, southern England, it is even possible to walk through the entire Mesozoic era – the age of the dinosaurs – by strolling along the beaches. Here the oldest Triassic rocks are 220 million years old. They do not yield many fossils; but there are later Jurassic and Cretaceous outcrops, too, and they are literally packed with remains.

Fossils are very commonly found by the sea in many regions; and one of the most extensive fossil-bearing deposits, dating back to 20-10 million years ago, lies on the east coast of North America at Calvert Cliffs, Maryland, where both professional collectors and beachcombers have found fossilized shark teeth, whale vertebrae, and other remains.

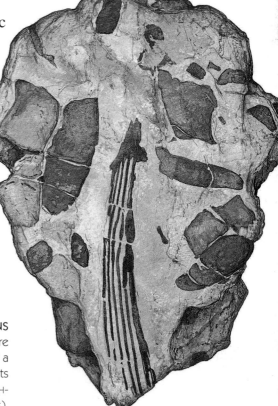

RARE REMAINS
In the piece of rock *right* are embedded the remains of a Jurassic shark known by scientists as *Hybodus cloasinus* (HEYE-BOH-DOOS KLOH-AR-EE-NUS).

AMATEUR FINDS

It is not only paleontologists who unearth fossils. Sometimes people without any knowledge of geology at all come across them entirely by accident in the strangest of places. They are probably not aware of what they have found until an expert takes a look.

In 1963 a rancher who had been working on an estate at a place called Muttaburra, in central Queensland, Australia, contacted the town's museum in great excitement.

FROM DOWN UNDER
When an Australian rancher found bones had become exposed in one of his fields due to weathering, he was thrilled to learn he had discovered the remains of a dinosaur.

On the banks of the Thomson River, where his cattle had been grazing, he had been amazed to find what looked like the bones of a dinosaur. He had been anxious to tell scientists about his discovery because the herd had already begun to scatter them.

What was more, he suspected that farmhands had been bold enough to sneak away with a few of the bones.

Sure enough, scientists were able to confirm that they were indeed the remains of a dinosaur, and after careful study it was found to be an entirely new and important species. After the remains of this 23-foot-long herbivore had been reconstructed, they dubbed it *Muttaburrasaurus langdoni* (MUT-AH-BUR-AH-SOR-US LANG-DOHN-EE). This is a combination of the name of the place where the bones had become exposed and the surname of the rancher who reported his discovery.

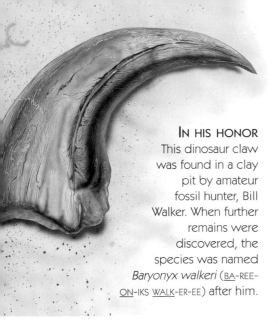

Farmers in China are even known to have come across dinosaur bones in their fields and, not realizing what they were, going ahead and using them to build pigsties! Farmers in the United State, meanwhile, have unwittingly used them as props and beams when building cabins. Indeed, this is how a major dinosaur site in Wyoming became known as Bone Cabin Quarry. Finally, 75 tons of dinosaur bones were dug up at this spot.

Many fragments of extinct species have in fact been discovered entirely by chance all over the world, even though, admittedly, it is usually paleontologists who know the most likely places to look. But recently, amateur enthusiast Lin Spearpoint was particularly fortunate.

Aware from the geology of the area that way back in Cretaceous times a deep river had existed in an area on the Isle of Wight off the south coast of England, she guessed that perhaps dinosaurs might have drowned in its waters and so asked a farmer whether she might dig on his land.

Her hunch proved right, and what she dug up were literally thousands of fragments of fossilized bone from one of the world's rarest dinosaurs, known as *Polacanthus*.

Fossilized teeth and pieces of skull have also been found by beachcombers, so it could be that you, too, may one day find some interesting remains.

In case that happens, be sure once again to remember the golden rules. First, it is never a good idea for anyone, even an adult, to go fossil hunting alone. You also always need permission to go onto and dig on private land. If remains do come to light, paleontologists emphasize that you should on no account attempt to dislodge them because they might easily be damaged. Instead, it is best to get in touch with a natural history museum and request its help.

Fact file

- The fossilized remains of extinct species can turn up in a whole variety of places – in fields, in caves, on beaches, or in mines, for example.

- If you would like to go fossil hunting, it is best to find out about membership of a local geological society and whether you could join an expedition.

- Amateurs have also found important trace fossils, such as 80-million-year-old tracks and coprolites.

- Hundreds of fossilized dinosaur eggs were found by a group of teenagers in central France entirely by chance.

- Anyone finding the fossilized remains of a new species may be fortunate enough to have it named after him or her by the scientists who study it.

If you tell them you think you have found some interesting fossils, they will almost certainly ask you to describe them, as well as the exact location; so if you can give a map reference, that will be helpful. If they think it could be worthwhile, they will visit the site; and depending on the rarity of what you have unearthed, the fossil may be dug up and put on display.

BONE WARS

Just as there was once a rush to western North America to find gold, so there was fierce competition among 19th-century paleontologists to find the richest fossil sites in the United States. Sometimes brawls even broke out over important remains.

The lengths to which many early paleontologists would go in the attempt to be the first to unearth the bones of new species of dinosaurs were almost beyond belief.

The famous paleontologist Edward Drinker Cope once pretended to be a traveler selling groceries, for instance, while he secretly spied on others to see what they had unearthed that day.

He also set out to destroy the reputation of his greatest rival, Othniel Marsh, by cultivating Marsh's assistants and then trying to turn them against their employer. But Marsh soon became suspicious and so refused access to his laboratory to all outsiders.

FISTICUFFS OVER FOSSILS
Men fought over new finds at important sites in Wyoming and Montana, as illustrated *below*. Meanwhile, counterfeit remains were planted as a false trail, and food supplies were frequently stolen in the attempt to sabotage a rival expedition.

TWO GREAT RIVALS

E.D. Cope, *left*, and O. Marsh, *right*, were bitter 19th-century rivals. They went out of their way to keep secret the sites of their proposed dinosaur digs and even set false trails, lest the other's team should manage to get there first and find valuable remains.

The situation grew even worse, however, when Cope made a terrible error in the reconstruction of a prehistoric marine reptile, and Marsh chose to mock him. (You can find out more about this famous mistake on page 37.)

By this time Marsh had become professor of paleontology at Yale, and Cope was based in Philadelphia, where he was studying the remains of carnivorous dinosaurs. Then, in 1877 Arthur Lakes, an amateur enthusiast, discovered a wealth of fossils in Colorado and sent some to Cope for analysis and some to Marsh.

Marsh immediately realized that this was an important find, and to prevent his rival, Cope, from getting in on the act, offered Lakes a bribe to keep the whole thing secret. Lakes promptly contacted Cope to request that he send the fossils to Marsh, and Cope was absolutely furious.

TIT FOR TAT

Meanwhile, another amateur enthusiast had unearthed equally interesting finds and sent them on to Cope. When Marsh got wind of this, he was equally annoyed, and so the ongoing game of tit for tat between these two great paleontologists grew more serious. Sometimes both would hire men especially to sabotage the other's sites, and false trails would be laid so that digging would start in an area where there were no fossils at all.

Each even set out to destroy the other. Over the years Cope had collected all the scandalous information he could get hold of about Marsh and managed to persuade the *New York Herald*, a leading newspaper, to publish an article about it all. Marsh's writings, he said, were stolen from other authors; he was accused of having wrongly identified a dinosaur bone as that of a buffalo; and he was branded a liar.

As a result of all this, Cope was nearly dismissed from his new professorship, and Marsh actually lost his post with the United States Geological Survey. But still their long-standing feud continued.

Marsh bequeathed his unsurpassed personal collection of fossils, then valued at well over $1 million (many times more in today's terms) to Yale University. Cope's collection was less substantial, and he sold it to the American Museum of Natural History. Would they perhaps have found even more exciting remains if they had combined forces instead of wasting time on rivalry?

Fact file

- Many of the fossil finds made during the Bone Wars are now on display in the United States in such major collections as the Smithsonian Institution, Washington D.C., the Peabody Museum at Yale, and the American Museum of Natural History, New York.

- During the 19th century expeditions to unearth fossils sometimes had to be postponed because of outbreaks of hostilities among the Native Americans.

- In 1897 O.C. Marsh received the highest award that can be given to a paleontologist – the Cuvier Prize presented once every three years and named after Baron Georges Cuvier, who had written *Researches on Fossil Bones* in 1812.

THE PALEOBOTANISTS

Botanists are scientists who study plant life as it is today. But there are also some who work alongside paleontologists and search for fossils of trees, shrubs, and flowers dating way back to prehistoric times. This profession is known as paleobotany.

The earliest plant fossils ever found date back about 430 million years; but flowering plants (classed as angiosperms and now the most common

IN EXPERT HANDS
This climbing swamp plant, an annularia, dates from Paleozoic times. The fossil is therefore at least 280 million years old. The specimen is from Italy.

form of flora on Earth) did not appear until the age of the dinosaurs, about 140 million years ago. Among them were species of magnolias and roses, similar in many ways to those with which we are familiar today. But some early plants were strange in appearance.

Indeed, morphology (examination of the structure of prehistoric plants, including their root systems, stems, leaves, and reproductive systems) is a very important part of a paleobotanist's work. He or she will also investigate the mutations (changes) in plant types over time and try to classify the fossils found into family groupings. The study of ancient pollen and spores, meanwhile, is known as palynology (PAL-IN-OL-OG-EE.)

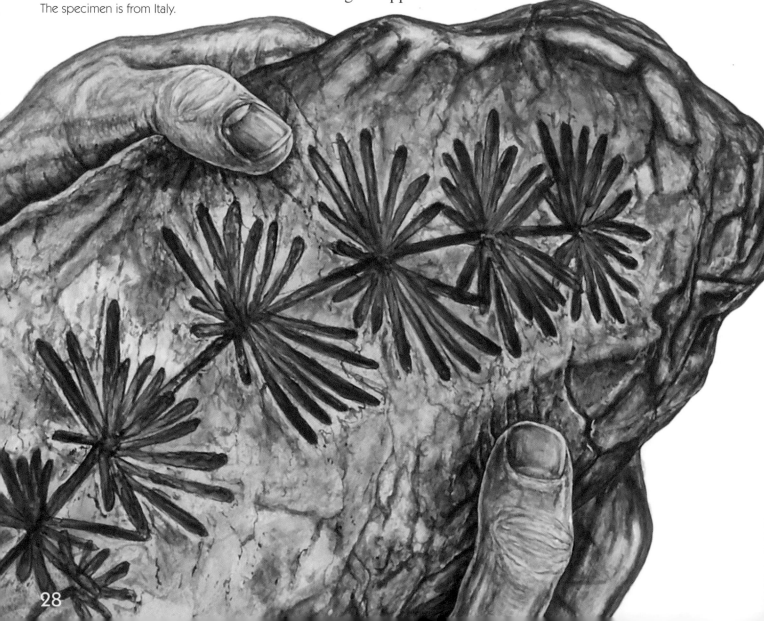

FOSSILIZED FRONDS
The fossilized plant, *left*, was unearthed in Queensland, Australia, and dates from Triassic times, when dinosaurs first evolved.

Through study of plant remains a lot about the history of the planet itself has been discovered. Indeed, ancient plants are excellent indicators of the climate in which they once lived. Over hundreds of thousands of years pollen in particular has proved to be extremely hardy, and the type of plants from which it came can often be identified with use of a powerful microscope. In fact, spores and pollen are known as microfossils because they can only be adequately viewed in this way.

Nevertheless, they are very commonly found, principally because they were produced in large quantities by plants and fungi. Ancient pollen has even been described by some paleobotanists as the best sort of window we have to past eras.

Fossilized foliage also holds secrets. Trees and shrubs having broad leaves and with long extensions for draining excess water, for example, most frequently grew in jungle.

Smaller leaves, however, often had a temperate forest origin, and tinier ones point to a more arid habitat. Perhaps you have yourself found the imprints of ancient plants in pieces of coal formed from petrified forests.

DIGGING DEEP

Where, though, are we most likely to find fossilized plants? These remains are most readily unearthed in what are known as badlands. They are dry areas that do not support much vegetation. Instead, they include numerous rocky outcrops. Fossilized bones sometimes become exposed out of the ground due to excessive weathering. Fossilized flora, however, tends to remain hidden under the surface, and so a considerable amount of careful probing is required. Indeed, hundreds of small holes may be dug in the course of a single day by a team of paleobotanists before they get lucky and find some interesting examples of fossilized vegetation. The age of the strata in which particular fossilized plants are discovered will naturally provide an indication of the time span during which they lived.

Fact file

- Paleobotany has a wide scope. It includes the study of ancient trees, ferns, shrubs, plants, algae, fungi, and bacteria.

- Through the work of paleobotanists we can predict how plant life might adapt in the long term if the present trend toward global warming continues.

- Dendrochronology (DEN-DROH-KRON-OL-OH-JEE) is the study of tree rings, through which the age of a fossilized tree when it died can be assessed, since most trees grow one new ring of tissue every year. This science can also reveal something about past climatic conditions. Thick rings are produced during warm, wet years, and thinner rings during drier or colder times.

FOOD FOR THE DINOSAURS
This extinct relative of the living maidenhair tree is 160-180 million years old and therefore not as ancient as the plant shown *above left*.

THE FOSSIL RECORD

Most paleontologists think that very primitive signs of life first appeared on Earth around 4.5 billion years ago, and that the human species did not evolve until far more recently. But how do they divide up the huge time span in between?

The chart *below* shows how the time for which life on our planet has existed is divided into five main eras. These are then broken down into 18 periods, each with a distinctive name, generally derived from the name of the place where rocks from that period were first exposed. The Devonian period, for example, is named after rocks in Devon, southern England; and the Jurassic period, after Europe's Jura Mountains.

DIGGING DEEP

The chart shown here, presented as a section through the Earth's crust, lists in the left-hand column the principal eras of our planet's history. In the right-hand column you will find listed the names of the periods into which each era is subdivided; while in the center column, headed MYA (meaning *millions of years ago*) we list the approximate time for which each period lasted. Note that in the chart the depth of each band is not proportional to the length of time it represents.

ERA	MYA	PERIOD
QUATERNARY (KWAT-ERN-A-REE) *Homo sapiens sapiens* evolves.	2 – PRESENT	**HOLOCENE** (HOL-OH-SEEN) **PLEISTOCENE** (PLEYE-STOH-SEEN)
CENOZOIC (SEN-OH-ZOH-IK) The first apes evolve, followed by early hominids. Horses and elephants appear, while existing species of mammals and birds start to spread.	22 – 2	**PLIOCENE** (PLEE-OH-SEEN) **MIOCENE** (MEYE-OH-SEEN) **OLIGOCENE** (OG-LEE-OH-SEEN)
	65 – 22	**EOCENE** (EE-OH-SEEN) **PALAEOCENE** (PAL-EE-PH-SEEN)
MESOZOIC (MEE-SOH-ZOH-IK) The earliest dinosaurs and small mammals appear in Triassic times and become extinct 65 million years ago.when flying reptiles and ammonites also disappear. Flowering plants date back to Cretaceous times. The planet's first birds appear in Jurassic times.	140 – 65	**CRETACEOUS** (CRET-AY-SEE-US)
	195 – 140	**JURASSIC** (JOOR-AS-IK)
	230 – 195	**TRIASSIC** (TREYE-AS-IK)
PALAEOZOIC (PAL-EE-OH-ZOH-IK) Huge forests cover the planet. Early reptiles appear.	280 – 230	**PERMIAN** (PERM-EE-AN)
	345 – 280	**CARBONIFEROUS** (KARB-ON-IF-ER-US)
Amphibians evolve. Ammonites, early sharks, armored fish, and gymnosperms appear.	395 – 345	**DEVONIAN** (DEV-OHN-EE-AN)
The first land plants and invertebrates appear.	435 – 395	**SILURIAN** (SEYEL-YOOR-EE-AN)
Corals and vertebrates evolve.	500 – 435	**ORDOVICIAN** (ORD-OH-VEE-SEE-AN)
Invertebrates, arthropods, sponges, and mollusks appear.	570 – 500	**CAMBRIAN** (KAM-BREE-AN)
ARCHAEOZOIC (ARK-EE-OH-ZOH-IK) Single-cell organisms visible to the naked eye start to evolve.		**ALGONIKIAN** (AL-GON-EEK-EE-AN) **ARCHAEAN** (ARK-EE-AN)
	4,500 – 570	

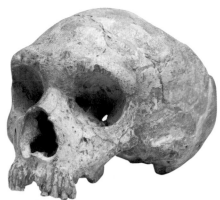

LONG GONE
Found in a quarry on the island of Gibraltar, this Neanderthal skull belonged to a female who lived about 50,000 years ago.

What caused the layers as shown on the chart *opposite* to form, however? Over literally thousands of millions of years our planet has been subject to enormous changes. Ocean depth fluctuated; the climate was sometimes extreme; many species died out, then others evolved; and all the while, many layers of different sorts of sedimentary rock, formed from the breakdown of other materials, were laid down, each containing the remains of life forms of that time. More recent sediments therefore lie above older strata, but any layer may become exposed at any time.

MIND THE GAP!

But our planet's geological past has always been dynamic. So even though sediments were laid down horizontally at first, over long periods uplift, erosion, or folding occasionally occurred, so that the rock patterns changed, and gaps were left not only in the Earth's strata but also in the fossil record. The great 19th-century British naturalist Charles Darwin, who called such gaps "unconformities," even believed they almost certainly represent longer periods of time than all the strata that are known to us.

When paleontologists find fossils of the same species in entirely different parts of the world, that provides an indication that these regions were once part of a larger land mass that eventually broke up so that identical life forms became separated. The remains of some Permian reptiles, dating from 250 million years ago, for example, have been found as far apart as South America, India, Antarctica, and southern Africa.

Fact file

- Index fossils are remains that have a wide geographical distribution and that therefore help paleontologists date rocks of a similar origin but situated far apart.

- Microfossils, such as pollen and spores, make very good index species.

- So-called pseudofossils (SOO-DOH-FOS-ILS), meaning "false fossils," date from very early times but may have misleading markings so that scientists risk making errors.

- The present layout of the world's continents did not arise until well into the Cenozoic era, also known as the Tertiary (TER-SEE-AR-EE), and commonly refered to as the age of the mammals because so many evolved at that time.

A DEVILISH-LOOKING DEVONIAN
The massive marine creature *above*, known as a *Dunklosteus* (DUNK-LOS-TEE-US), dates from 350 million years ago and is illustrated with some early sharks.

OLD BUT NOT FORGOTTEN!
The fossil fish shown *left* was found in strata at Lyme Regis, southern England, that showed paleontologists it must be about 150 million years old.

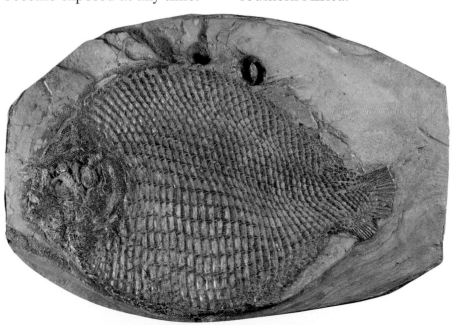

EXCAVATING BONES

Fossilized remains are continually found in virtually every country of the world. But the ways in which they are removed vary according to the size of each specimen. In general, the bigger the creature, the more difficult it is to extract.

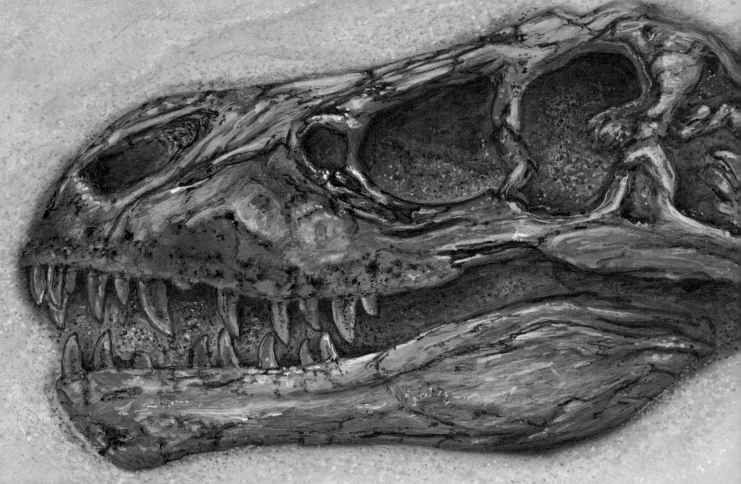

A GRADUAL PROCESS
The photograph *above* shows a fossilized rhino skeleton being painstakingly removed from the ground by a team of paleontologists.

For 170 million years or thereabout the skeleton of a magnificent Jurassic meat-eating dinosaur had lain buried deep in a quarry in Sichuan Province, central China, before it was discovered.

No one knows how this creature died – of natural causes, perhaps; from disease; following some cataclysmic event; or after having been overcome by an even larger and fiercer predator.

We can assume, though, that for a long while after its flesh had decomposed, the skull and vertebrae of this 13-foot-long carnivore looked as they do in the illustration across these two pages before becoming fossilized and broken up by the ravages of time. Imagine, then, how methodical the paleontologists had to be in removing all the pieces from the ground. It was a an extraordinarily difficult job.

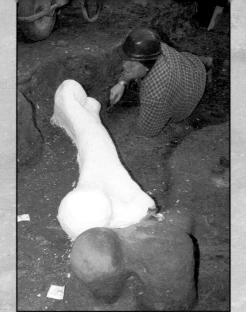

GETTING PLASTERED
The woolly mammoth femur (thigh bone), *right,* is seen being removed from its excavation site in Norfolk, England. It has been encased in plaster for protection.

FROM THE TOP

It can sometimes take several months to extract a single large fossil from the rock that surrounds it at a site. On a cliff face, for example, any rock overlying the specimen will first have to be removed, using picks, jackhammers, or even explosives if the rock above the fossil is extremely deep and turns out to be impenetrable.

Ideally, around 2.5 inches of rock will be left above the specimen, so that it can then be slowly and carefully chipped away with a suitable tool and a steady hand.

A SICK THEORY

But among the most bizarre fossilized remains ever found and removed for study and possible eventual display is fossilized vomit, found in a clay quarry in Peterborough, England. At an international conference held in Denmark at the start of 2002 it was announced by its discoverers that this pile of partly digested shells, etched away by stomach acid, had probably been thrown up by a marine monster some 160 million years ago!

BONE BEDS
Utah is home to many dinosaur bone beds like the one *below.* Unearthing such remains requires delicate work to ensure the valuable fossil evidence remains intact.

33

UNEARTHING EGGS

Who would have thought that anyone would ever find eggs laid by dinosaurs way back in Cretaceous times! What is more, through use of special X-ray techniques paleontologists have even found evidence of growing embryos inside them. So why did they fail to hatch?

ANCIENT NESTING SITES
The 90-million-year-old dinosaur eggs shown here were layed by a *Protoceratops* (<u>PROH</u>-TOH-<u>SER</u>-AH-TOPS) and formed part of a nesting site unearthed in Mongolia's Gobi Desert. They were oval and found close by the skeletal remains of adults of this species. In other nearby nests scientists found round eggs and assume they would have hatched into another type of dinosaur. In 1978 palaeontologists Bob Makela and Jack Horner made the equally amazing discovery of the nesting site of another type of dinosaur, a *Maiasaura* (<u>MEYE</u>-AH-<u>SOR</u>-AH), in Montana.

Roy Chapman Andrews and his team were absolutely astounded. There in the rock were the remains of a whole clutch of fossilized eggs.

Soon they found several nests in the area, all containing elongated eggs laid in neatly arranged, circular formations.

The expedition, organized by the American Museum of Natural History, had set off for Mongolia in 1922 to search for early human remains, since Andrews was (wrongly) convinced that *Homo sapiens* must first have evolved in Asia.

No such remains were finally unearthed. But finding these eggs had more than made up for the initial disappointment.

PROOF AT LAST
Imagine the wonder and excitement when Roy Chapman Andrews and his team made their extraordinary find! Before this discovery paleontologists wrongly believed dinosaurs might have been mammals, giving birth to live young.

They proved to be among the very first fossilized eggs ever identified as having been laid by dinosaurs and as such were a landmark discovery, even though some experts suspect dinosaur eggs may have come to light many thousands of years ago and fragments of shell were used for decorative jewelry by primitive peoples.

A few dinosaur eggs had in fact been unearthed and identified in France a few years prior to Andrews' expedition. But Andrews' finds, at an area known colloquially as Flaming Cliffs because of the local bright pink sandstone, were the first to include entire nests. The eggs inside them, meanwhile, have been described as resembling large baked potatoes!

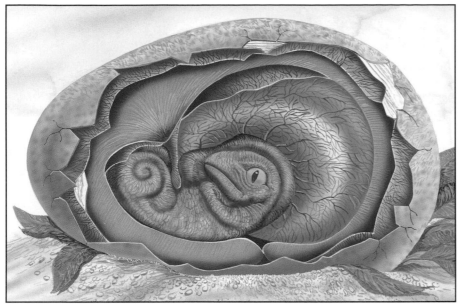

A CRACKING FIND
Using advanced scanning techniques, scientists have been able
to examine the contents of a fossilized dinosaur egg, shown *above*,
70 million years after it was laid. The embryo that died is clearly visible.

Andrews' team found other remarkable remains, too, when they made further expeditions to the Gobi, among them *Oviraptor* (OV-EE-RAP-TOR), a beaked, birdlike dinosaur given a name meaning "egg thief" but now actually believed to have died there while protecting its own eggs.

INSIDE INFORMATION

Over the years a great many other egg finds have been made in places as far apart as Uruguay, Romania, India, and North America. But especially exciting was the discovery, in 1995, by another team of American palaeontologists of an egg of the Cretaceous herbivore *Saltasaurus* (SALT-AH-SOR-US) from Argentina. It was in excellent condition, and a scan revealed that tucked away inside the egg were the remains of an embryo that had died at a very early stage of its development.

Evidence of a baby *Oviraptor* has also been found within the partly worn-away shell of a fossilized egg. Lots of fragments of shell have been discovered, too. But why did some dinosaur eggs never hatch? No one is entirely sure, although some scientists have suggested they may not have been adequately incubated. Dinosaurs would often bury their eggs in the sand after covering them with vegetation for extra protection and warmth. But adverse weather conditions or disease may have arisen, or predators may have chased away those mothers incubating the eggs themselves.

Fossil evidence also shows that some dinosaurs would lay their eggs in straight lines, while others laid in a very distinct circular formation.

Although a great many dinosaur eggs have been unearthed, they still command a high price; and natural history collections, as well as private collectors, are always eager to acquire new specimens, although in most cases we will never know the species that might have been born.

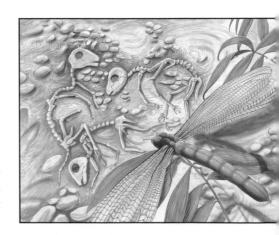

PINT-SIZED
Some baby dinosaurs, such as this *Mussaurus* (MUS-OR-OSS) seem to have been very small when they first hatched.

FAMOUS MISTAKES

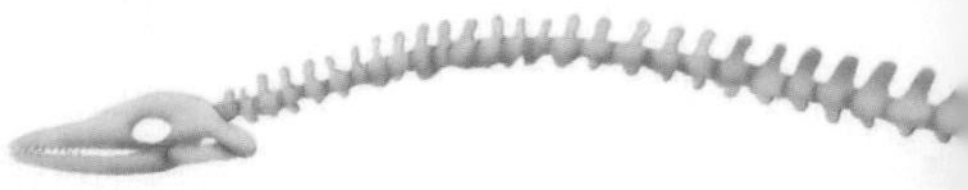

Even experts sometimes make an error when reconstructing the skeleton of an extinct creature, occasionally with amusing results. But it has also been known for such mistakes to be encouraged.

AT THE WRONG END
Putting together skeletal remains is no easy task, particularly when the creature is as elongated as the plesiosaur shown here. So perhaps it is not too surprising that this prehistoric marine creature's head was initially placed on its tail.

In the past, and perhaps even today, in the attempt to hoodwink the public and also their colleagues, paleontologists and taxidermists have provided incorrect information by "inventing" a species and then presenting its bogus remains, as if to test how gullible or knowledgeable people are. But genuine errors can be made. Back in the 17th century, for example, a professor at Oxford University, Robert Plot, had been presented with a most extraordinary fossil.

Plot's opinion was that it might have been the thigh bone of some enormous elephant, brought to England by the Romans, though he admitted that there were no written records of these creatures ever having been brought to the British Isles. But he finally decided it was a bone from some member of a giant race of humans that had once existed, and it was wrongly labeled in one of his works as a *scrotum humanum*, or human scrotum! Now we know, however, that it was part of a skeleton of a *Megalosaurus* (MEG-AH-LOH-SOR-US), a species of dinosaur.

Another major mistake was made when the highly respected anatomist Sir Richard Owen, one of the best known scientists of his day, helped make a restoration of a dinosaur.

NOT WHAT IT SEEMS
If anyone tells you the jackalope once existed, as shown here, take it with a pinch of salt. It was created as a practical joke by scientists who placed a deer's antlers on top of a hare's head!

36

Owen felt this dinosaur must have looked like a rhinoceros and so assumed it probably had a nose horn. A bone was therefore placed on the skull of the *Iguanodon* (IG-WAHN-OH-DON), but it was soon found that this fossil was actually *Iguanodon's* spiked thumb.

When paleontologists first put together the bones of a *Tsintaosaurus* (SIN-TAY-OH-SOR-US) – a 33-foot-long duck-billed dinosaur found in China – they decided one piece of bone they had unearthed must have been a tall spike that stuck up from its head. But scientists now believe that this long bone was simply a piece from the skull's surface that had broken away.

Differences of opinion can also arise at times among paleontologists. Rivalry between the two great American dinosaur hunters O.C. Marsh and E. D. Cope, for instance, was made worse when Marsh sneered at Cope for placing a plesiosaur's head on the end of its tail.

TONGUE IN CHEEK?

Dubious theories have also been put forward about what led to the demise of the dinosaurs. Among them is the outlandish idea that they all died of rickets as a result of a severe mineral deficiency; but there is no evidence at all to back this up.

The Hungarian dinosaur enthusiast Baron Nopsca, however, said he was not joking when he declared all duck-billed dinosaurs with crests were males. But it was pure guesswork on his part, and paleontologists now know this was certainly not the case.

LOST PLOT
At first, 17th-century museum keeper Robert Plot thought the strange fossil, *left*, now lost, belonged to a giant human ancestor, but we now know it was part of the dinosaur *Megalosaurus* (MEG-AH-LOH-SOR-US.)

A HORNY PROBLEM
Scientists first decided the dinosaur *Tsintaosaurus* must have had a horn, but we now know it had a smooth head, as shown *above*.

IN THE LABORATORY

There are skeletal remains of thousands of different prehistoric creatures on view in all the world's natural history museums. But a great deal of preparation was required before these bones were finally ready for reconstruction and display to the public.

Fossils are valuable items. So as soon as they have been dug up, they will be wrapped by experts and then carefully transported to a museum laboratory.

SPECIAL TREATMENT
An acid bath, a chisel, brushes, and a microscope – these are just some of the many tools used in museum laboratories, such as the one illustrated *below*.

In many respects this sort of laboratory resembles a high-tech workshop in which you would find a strong workbench with clean surfaces, good lighting, a wide variety of chemicals, computers, powerful microscopes, and a wide range of other tools, including soft brushes, drills, and chisels.

A CLEAN START
Whatever their size, fossils are very delicate. It is vital that, after having been buried for thousands or even millions of years, these ancient remains do not become damaged as soon as humans come into contact with them.

So once in the lab, large fossils are clamped into place to keep them from slipping, Then they are slowly and gently cleaned, using a magnifying glass or even a microscope for closeup views of their surfaces.

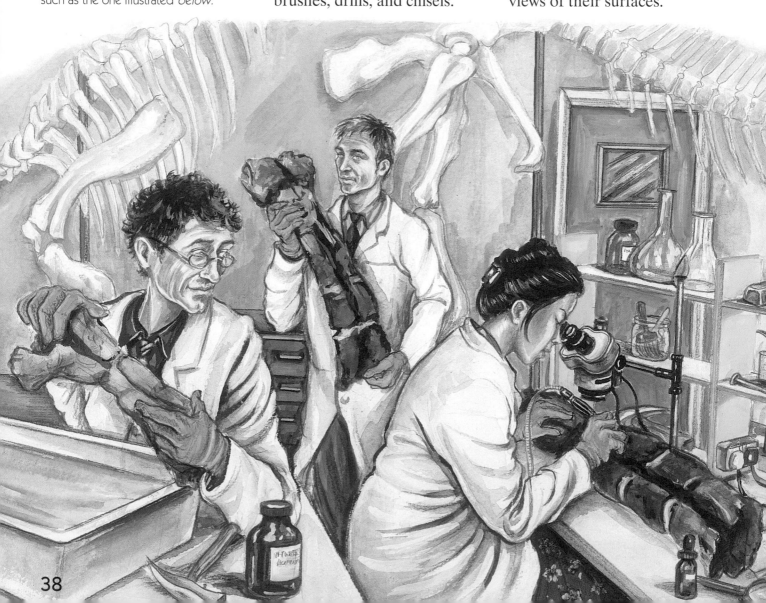

FINE WORK
In the photograph *above*, a paleontologist is using a rotary diamond-edged dental saw to work at the hard rock surrounding a dinosaur fossil.

The cleaning process will remove chalk, clay, or shale and can be carried out by hand, using either a thin needle or a hard chisel, depending on the state and size of the remains. But often a brush dipped in water or detergent will be sufficient to dislodge most of the dirt. Sometimes, however, a small drill will be used, or a sandblaster may be brought in to blow away unwanted dust. Special ultrasonic devices that can dislodge particles of dirt when a fossil is placed in water are an alternative.

When the fossil is softer than the rock in which it has become embedded, more advanced methods may be required. In this case a technician will generally place the fossil in an acid bath to strip away the layers of rock – known as the "matrix" – around the bone.

Hydrochloric and acetic acids are commonly used, but the choice of which acid to use depends on the type of fossil.

Another cleaning method involves a process known as erosion or etching. It is particularly useful when many small bones need to be extracted from a large lump of rock. Any exposed parts are first painted with an acid-resistant glue, and the entire fossil will then be placed in an acid solution. Great care must be taken because the chemicals involved can be flammable or burn the skin.

Working with acid is certainly risky. Rubber gloves and eye protectors are therefore worn, and fossils are washed after use of chemicals. Such laboratories are always well ventilated, too; otherwise noxious fumes may become overpowering.

Gradually, more of the fossil will break free of the rock matrix; and after it has been washed and allowed to dry, the process is repeated several times until every layer of matrix has been removed.

But the matrix can also be dislodged in other ways – by heating the fossil in an oven, for example, or by boiling.

Sometimes the laboratory technicians will find tiny holes in bones, but they are never eliminated. Indeed, they could provide important clues for later reconstruction of the remains. They may mark, for instance, the original position of major blood vessels, muscles, and nerves.

Fact file

- There may be hundreds or even thousands of bones to study and sort under laboratory conditions after a major dig.

- Bones need careful, dry storage while they are being examined. It will prevent them from becoming eroded by exposure to excessive moisture in the air.

- Paleontologists sometimes paint resin on crumbling fossils to keep them from breaking up as they are being unearthed prior to work in the laboratory.

- Microfossils, such as teeth, can be separated from surrounding material by floating them in an oily or salty solution. The fossil floats, and the debris will sink.

A LONG, SLOW PROCESS

Some of these cleaning processes can take many months; and as might be expected with fragile remains, accidents occasionally happen.

If so, repairs will be carried out with a special glue, or resin. If it proves adequate, the lab technicians will finally provide a full written account for the museum, listing every stage of what has taken place.

Such reports may be useful in the future in case other scientists want to know which chemicals and methods were used on a particular fossil in its original state. Specimens are now ready for reconstruction and eventual display.

RECONSTRUCTIONS

Some large skeletons of extinct creatures on display in museums today are actually fiberglass replicas. But how do paleontologists set about putting together the original bones unearthed in the course of a dig so they can then make these lightweight copies?

The first step in rebuilding a fossilized skeleton is for all the bones to be placed in the correct order, even if some are missing. This is not easy, however, and may require complex and time-consuming detective work. If there is any doubt, paleontologists will look carefully at other reconstructed skeletons of the same species or study the anatomy of creatures of a similar type.

Marks are sometimes present on the fossiized bones, and they provide an accurate indication not only as to where muscles were attached but the size of the creature's muscles, but also how much flesh there is likely to have been on the body.

To help put a large skeleton together, paleontologists also often make use of a specially built steel framework known as an armature.

The animal's leg bones will be put in position on the armature first. Then the spine and the ribs can be added, and finally the skull and tail. Any missing bones, meanwhile, will be replaced with fiberglass replicas so that the skeleton is complete.

IN SUSPENSE

But some creatures are now reconstructed in another way. Instead of the fossilized bones being supported from below, steel wires are used to suspend them individually from the ceiling, so that the final effect is much like the body of a giant string puppet.

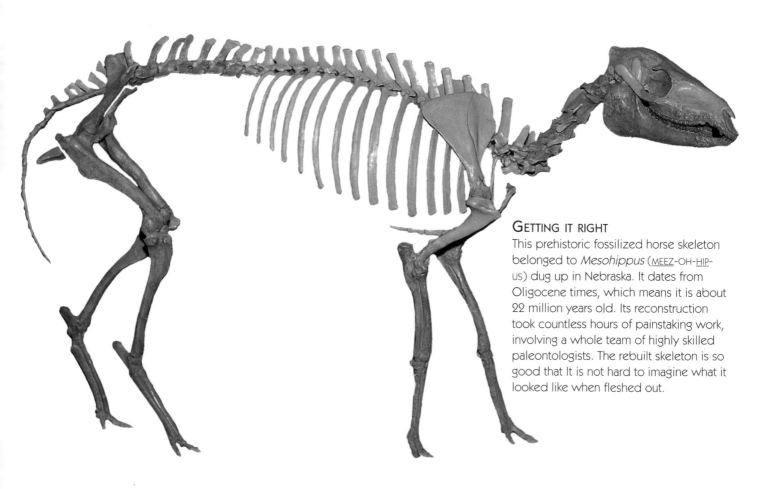

GETTING IT RIGHT
This prehistoric fossilized horse skeleton belonged to *Mesohippus* (MEEZ-OH-HIP-US) dug up in Nebraska. It dates from Oligocene times, which means it is about 22 million years old. Its reconstruction took countless hours of painstaking work, involving a whole team of highly skilled paleontologists. The rebuilt skeleton is so good that It is not hard to imagine what it looked like when fleshed out.

GETTING AHEAD

It is bound to take considerable time for palentologists to reconstruct all the bones of a huge, 5-ton, plant-eating dinosaur known by the scientific name *Nigersaurus* (NEYE-JER-SOR-US) that was found recently in remarkably complete condition in Niger, Africa. The head alone has been a great challenge because scientists think it must be the toothiest species ever found. In all, it had more than 1,000 teeth, as many as 10 emerging from single points in the upper and lower jaws. They would have helped it cope with huge quantities of vegetation, which is why it has been given the amusing popular name of Lawnmower, even though grass is said not to have existed at the time this creature walked what is now Africa's Sahara Desert about 140 million years ago.

The fossilized bones of a sauropod dinosaur *Barosaurus* (BAR-OH-SOR-US), meanwhile, lay in storage at the American Museum of Natural History for 60 years before technicians got around to assembling this giant jigsaw puzzle. Fortunately, however, the bones had been numbered, providing clues as to where each belonged.

Amazingly, this magnificent skeleton was reconstructed so that it would be seen on display at the museum rearing up on its hind legs. But replica bones were used, so molds first had to be made by painting the actual fossils with liquid rubber.

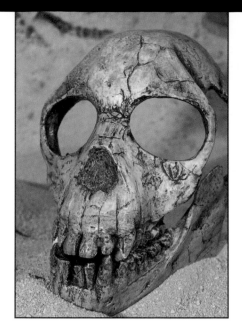

SPOT THE DIFFERENCE!
Sometimes remains are so fragile that paleontologists prefer to put a fiberglass replica on display, as was the case with a *Proconsul* skull, *above*, from Africa.

Each bone was molded in two halves; and once they had dried, these flexible, hollow shapes could then be peeled away to be filled with liquid plastic. Later, the outer layer was removed so that the replica bones could be painted to resemble the original fossils. Sometimes, however, very sparse fossil evidence is unearthed for a species. There is then no alternative for scientists but to assess what the creature would have looked like from, say, just a few teeth. In such instances, though, they will usually simply sketch what they think the creature would have looked like instead of building a complete replica.

But from now on, fleshed-out reconstructions of dinosaurs may never again look the same because a paleontologist at Ohio University suspects their nostrils should be placed far forward, just above the mouth, and not on top of their heads,

ALL TOGETHER NOW
The huge *Tyrannosaurus rex* skull *above*, seen being examined by a museum visitor, was in pieces when found, but experts succeeded in reassembling it.

giving them an excellent sense of smell. Existing models may therefore have to be altered accordingly.

FORTUNATE FINDS

Perseverance, initiative, an eager eye, a sound knowledge of geology, and a sprinkling of good luck – these are just some of the elements that combine to make important discoveries, as you will gather from the accounts that follow.

David Baldwin was not a professional paleontologist, working only as an occasional assistant on 19th-century digs.

FOLLOWING IN HIS FOOTSTEPS
The illustration *below* shows two paleontologists unearthing further finds at the New Mexico site where David Baldwin had first made his momentous discovery.

Yet he went on to make one of the most fascinating discoveries of his time.

Baldwin had often helped the well-known paleontologist Othniel C. Marsh, but later turned to lending a hand to that man's great rival, Edward D. Cope. However, he always refused to be part of any team.

Stubborn, his preference was to dig independently if he could and then send back any finds for expert identification.

EARLY REMAINS
So it was that in 1881, having personally unearthed a few rather scrappy remains in Triassic rocks in New Mexico, Baldwin decided to send them to Cope, who immediately recognized them as belonging to the small, lightly built carnivorous dinosaur *Coelophysis* (SEEL-OH-FEYE-SIS.)

GETTING IT RIGHT

These dinosaur bones – bits of leg, vertebrae, pelvis, and ribs – did not in any way make up a complete skeleton, however; so Cope assumed they must have belonged to three different types of *Coelophysis*. Later, though, he was to be proved wrong. Cope had mistaken what were actually three different ages and sizes of the single species *Coelophysis* for three different species of this particular dinosaur. Baldwin's find had indeed been a momentous one and was to lead to further important discoveries.

BY THE DOZEN

Good fossil hunters always bear in mind how vital it is either to scour a site repeatedly, even if only one interesting find had been made there. So, many years later an expedition returned to the spot in New Mexico where Baldwin had originally been so successful, and which had since become part of an estate with the mysterious name Ghost Ranch.

This new dig proved very worthwhile, too, since many further remains of this Triassic dinosaur were unearthed. In fact, on excavating a hillside, they discovered several dozen skeletons in all. They are now known to be the remains of many dinosaurs of the same species – both adult and juvenile specimens of *Coelophyis* – that had probably perished together in some sort of flash flood.

THE FATHER OF PALEONTOLOGY
This portrait of the 19th-century scientist Sir Richard Owen, dubbed the father of paleontology, shows him holding the leg bone of a moa dug up in New Zealand.

But sometimes it is very unexpected people who are responsible for major finds. After he became president of the United States in 1800, Thomas Jefferson maintained his interest in science and determined to promote a dig, led by General William Clark, at the so-called Big Bone Lick in Kentucky. Ultimately, more than 300 bones, most of them the remains of mammoths, were found there.

LUCKY LADY
Mary Ann Mantell, wife of the 19th-century British doctor and scientist Gideon Mantell, was strolling in Sussex, England, when she suddenly caught sight of a tooth embedded in rock. Mary immediately took it to her husband, who described it as a *"large tooth which, from the worn, smooth, and oblique surface of the crown, had evidently belonged to an herbivorous animal."* The rock had originally been removed from a local quarry, and a number of bones were found there, too – all later identified as *Iguanodon* remains, thanks to Mary's very prompt action.

Fact file

- Sir Richard Owen, who first coined the word "dinosaur," was given the nickname "Old Bones" because of his interest in paleontology

- It was the observant 19th-century British scientist Thomas H. Huxley who first noticed a similarity in bone structure between dinosaurs and birds when studying the remains of the 2-foot-long Jurassic dinosaur known as *Compsognathus* (COMP-SOG-NAY-THUS). Indeed, most paleontologists now agree birds are probably descended from the dinosaurs.

- Fossilized impressions of dinosaur skin are very rare, but some were discovered in the 19th century by the American Charles Sternberg and his three sons.

Jefferson was so proud of this achievement that he actually turned one of the rooms in the White House into a museum for displaying the fossils to his visitors.

PRIME SITES

Sometimes just a few animal fossils are found in one location. But occasionally a whole wealth of remains are unearthed in one spot. This is usually because some sort of catalcysmic event happened there, so that many animals perished together.

London, England, is one of the world's biggest and busiest modern cities. So it was entirely unexpected when, in 1957, workmen who were digging on a building site in Trafalgar Square, right in the heart of the metropolis, suddenly found a few fossils. They immediately called in the experts.

A TERRIBLE END
In a section of Los Angeles known as Rancho La Brea paleontologists found the remains of about 2,000 saber-toothed tigers and many other prehistoric animals that had perished in a tar pit.

What these paleontologists then discovered right by the square's fountains and the landmark of Nelson's Column, (built in honor of the great 19th-century British naval commander who fought in the Battle of Waterloo) were countless remains of such prehistoric creatures as cave lions, an ancestor of the elephant known as *Palaeoloxodon* (<u>PAL</u>-EYE-OH-<u>LOX</u>-OH-DON), ancient hippos and hyenas, wild boar, and giant deer and cattle.

None of these creatures lives in England nor any other part of Great Britain today. How long ago, then, did they inhabit that region? And how might they all have died together about 100,000 years ago, when marshes lined the Thames?

BIT BY BIT
When paleontologists first find evidence of an extensive bone bed, like the one *above* in Alberta, Canada, they know they must work slowly but surely at uncovering the remains.

This river was even wider in prehistoric times than it is now, and lots of these animals came there to drink or bathe. Scientists think these remains show they may have become the victims of a flood of some kind, and some may even have been washed down from surrounding hills to what is now Trafalgar Square by fast-flowing rivers and streams.

But London is not the only busy center to have become a prime fossil site. Part of Los Angeles known as Rancho La Brea has also yielded thousands of fossilized remains, so that we know creatures such as mammoths, giant ground sloths, and saber-toothed tigers once roamed there.

GIANT DIG
Dr. Werner Janensch, who led expeditions to Africa during which important remains of *Brachiosaurus* were discovered, is shown *right*, posing with some of his hundreds of helpers and one of the giant sauropod's bones.

MONUMENTAL FINDS

Between 1909 and 1912, at a town called Tendaguru in Tanzania, Africa, the curator of the Humboldt Museum, Berlin, Germany, and his team found hundreds of tons of bones belonging to nine species of dinosaurs, among them a spectacular *Brachiosaurus* (BRAK-EE-OH-SOR-OOS), for almost 200 years the longest complete skeleton in the world.

Earlier, in 1886, when coal and oil were extracted from a huge pit at Messel, Germany, scientists had also found fossilized evidence of the sort of animals that had existed in this region between 64 and 2 million years ago when Europe had a climate much like that of Florida today. Indeed, it seems anteaters, tapirs, pangolins, and antelopes, now extinct in that part of the world, once thrived there.

But whether or not in millions of years time our descendants find prime sites providing fossilized evidence

Fact file

● At a place known as the Fort Union Formation in the Crazy Mountain Basin of Montana fossils of 70 different species of prehistoric mammals have been unearthed, including early primates. Fossilized amphibians, crustacea, and plants have also been discovered there.

● Many fascinating fossils probably await discovery in the Gobi Desert, which is partly in China and partly in Mongolia. That is because the desert sandstone has remained undisturbed for many millions of years.

● Huge numbers of bones belonging to prehistoric giant marsupials (pouched mammals) have been found in lakes and caves in many parts of Australia.

for many creatures of today that to them will be entirely unfamiliar depends to a great extent how kindly we treat our wildlife heritage now.

GLOSSARY

ammonite
an extinct soft-bodied aquatic
creature with a coiled shell

arid
dry (describing either soil or
the climate)

arthropods
a group of invertebrates with
jointed bodies, including
insects and spiders

carnivore
a meat-eater

Cretaceous times
a period lasting from about 144
to 65 million years ago

decompose
to rot

embryo
an early stage of a mammal's
development before birth

erosion
wearing away

evolve
to change over time

fronds
large leaves

gastropods
a group of creatures including
snails, slugs, whelks, and others

habitat
the environment in which a
creature lives

herbivore
a plant-eater

hibernate
to sleep thoughout the cold
season

hominid
an early humanlike creature

igneous
describes rocks derived from
volcanic lava

incubate
to sit on or warm eggs so that
they hatch

Jurassic times
a period lasting from about 213
to 144 million years ago

limestone
a type of rock mainly made up
of the mineral calcium
carbonate

magnetic field
a field of force around a
permanent magnet, such as the
center of the Earth

oasis
a fertile area in the desert

organism
a living plant or animal

paleontologist
a scientist who studies fossils

permafrost
permanently frozen ground

petrified
turned to stone

phosphate
any of several chemicals
containing the mineral
phosphorus

polyurethane
a type of plastic

pterosaur
a prehistoric flying reptile

sauropod
one of many Jurassic long-
necked, plant-eating dinosaurs

sedimentary rocks
rocks containing several layers

spelunker
someone who explores caves

strata
layers

taxidermist
an expert in preserving dead
creatures

theropods
a predatory group of dinosaurs,
mostly bipedal (two-legged)

Triassic times
a period lasting from about 249
to 213 million years ago

titanosaur
a type of dinosaur

trilobite
a small extinct marine creature